Communication Skills for Workplace Success

How to Practice Effective Communication in Work & Life, Boost Your Income & Thrive Effectively

By

Joshua Strachan

Other Books by the Same Author

Thank you for purchasing this book. As you become equipped to be a winner in every aspect of life, below are other books you should add to your library—to learn new skills and develop the motivation to push beyond yourself:

- Persuasion Psychology: How to Influence People (Master the Art of Power and Mind Control Techniques)
- Emotional Intelligence: How to Improve Your IQ, Achieve Self-Awareness and Control Your Emotions
- Happiness Hack: The Beginner's Guide to Happiness
- The Creative Treasures: 100 Creative Ways to Boost Your Creativity, Gain Recognition and Establish Authority
- Memory Improvement Techniques: How to Develop a Brilliant Memory, Recall Things Faster and Achieve a Speedy Learning Ability

- [The S.M.A.R.T. Goals:](#) How to Get Rich with No Money or Education
- [How to Analyze People:](#) "Reading Body Language Psychology" To Recognize Personality Patterns, Understand People And Gain Influence
- [61 Ways to Attract Women According to 61 Experts:](#) The Ultimate Seduction Guide to Become the Alpha Male Women Can't Resist, Unlock Her Legs and Make them Fall in Love
- [How to Become Successful in Life:](#) Motivational Self Help for Wealth Creation and Life Strategies
- [Secrets to a Successful Long-Term Relationship:](#) The Key to a Passionate Marriage and Sex Life
- [Self-Discipline Training](#): Ways to Develop Self-Discipline & Stay Committed to A Routine, No Matter What
- [How to Organize Your Life:](#) 10 Habits of Really Organized People
- [The Law of Attraction Workbook:](#) How to Attract Abundance of Money, Wealth, Love & Health (Turn Failure into Success)

- <u>Time Management Made Easy:</u> **How to** Cultivate New Habits, Improve Productivity & Get Things Done

Table of Contents

Introduction 6

How to Communicate Effectively 9

The Feedback System 11

Giving and Getting 14

The Art of Mindedness 16

Using Empathic Power 18

The Art of Approach 20

Fraternize Effectively 22

Clarity and Concision 24

Hone Your Nonverbal Communication 26

The Better Listener 29

Get Rid of Distractions 32

Use Script 33

Other Books by the Same Author 34

Introduction

The success of your business and social life depends on your ability to communicate effectively with the right people. In fact, your personality, intelligence and potentials can be detected through the simple ways you express yourself.

Even in workplace, communication becomes a tool for success that the level of your breakthrough could ultimately be determined by the level of smartness you exhibit through your communication. This brings about the importance of learning effective communication in order to expand your potential for success both in business and personal relationships.

Even in sending messages or emails concerning a preposition or promotion, your mode of communication affects the kind of respond you get. This book is dedicated for teaching explicit communication skills that will land you greater opportunities in the workplace and outside the office. Different effective communication tactics have been releveled to help you learn and adopt to the 21st century ways of achieving greater things through mere verbal and nonverbal communication.

Good communication skills ultimately determine the level of the quality of relationship a person is capable of cultivating. It involves how you are being understood and how much you are able to convince people about your innovation and ideas. The value of what you brought to the table will be determined by how well you present it through effective communication.

How to Communicate Effectively

Pick The Right Medium

Communication is not just about having a conversation; it is also about picking the right medium for conversing effectively. Most people make the mistake of using random means just to get to someone but it is important that you choose an effective medium based on the entire purpose of the communication.

Beginning from email, texts, phone call, face to face conversation, to writing a note or letter, you should be thinking of the perfect way to convey your message, the way it would have the desired effect on the receiver. So ultimately it is not always about the massage but the medium by which the message is being conveyed.

Studies have shown that the same people might respond to the same message differently when the message medium are modified. The medium changes the tone of the message, determines mutuality, and ultimately how important it is to the sender. So the response of the receiver is invariably modified.

The Feedback System

Demand Feedback

You should strive to seek feedback on the effect of your communication skills. Communication is not a general phenomenon that could be determined just by how important the message is to you. Different people in different places and different circumstances interpret messages differently. They communicate differently because they have varied priorities. They see you differently because of the kind of relationship you are having.

It is of great importance that you find effective ways to get a feedback from your employees or employer in order to determine your level of effectiveness. It would also help your communication skills positively even as you learn better ways to express yourself. Even when it comes to a work process, you should never keep a closed ear to the comments of people that know better.

Your success might be ultimately determined by the amount and relevance of criticism you receive, and how you make good use of them. Even as they communicate their motivations, their points of view, and suggest ways you can do better, it is only important that you listen and accept. If someone is not clear about things you said or some processes you initiated, take the time to explain further to them even as you create satisfaction in the atmosphere. With this practices you will hone your communication skills and finding effectiveness will become natural all of a sudden.

Giving and Getting

Respect

In order to speak and get people to listen and do as you say, you must be respected. And the easiest way to get respect is by actually giving respect. Most people misinterpret respect with fear. So they consistently make effort to apply reactions and tricks that will make people fear them instead of trying to make people to respect them.

The difference between fear and respect is very clear. If someone respects you, they will try as much as possible to respect your values even in your absence, but if someone only fears you, your values are useless when they are not under your supervision. Another way of gaining respect is by listening to people when they speak about their interests. Make eye contacts and use their names often to make them feel important.

Do not use your phone while having a conversation with them, and if you have an important phone call, excuse yourself politely, and always come back once done. Respect could also be determined by the quality of message you send to people. For example, a well-written and edited email brings about more prospects than a shabby written message. The person senses the time you take to edit and write well, and feels respected automatically.

The Art of Mindedness

Be Open Minded

Open mindedness becomes a crucial part of effective communication. When you are open you also allow other people to be open without the fear of disclosing too much information to you. Try as much as possible to make people trust you on the details they share with you. When you have such effect, you can be able to influence them by the things you say because they will acknowledge how much you know about them as the determinant for your decisions. When you are open-minded, you understand people better and this will hone your communication skills to the utmost.

Knowing more about your audience will help you to use better punch words, better tones and better medium for effective communication.

Also, you should exercise the patience of having to converse with people you often disagree with. Yes, you can argue all the time but you have to make sure that you understand their points of view so that you would speak from their perspectives, even if you have to show different judgment.

Using Empathic Power

Empathy

Empathy is simply the quality of understanding people as they are. It is the ability to read and understand people's emotions and respond to them effectively.

Empathy is one of the most important social skills in the 21st century. People need to know that you understand them before they will be open to you. The amount of effect you would have depends on the amount of empathy you display.

Everyone is struggling to be understood, and regardless of a person's rank or social status there is this constant need for approval within every human. Serve the need for humanity by showing that you respect and understand the point of view of the people you are communicating with. This would also determine and show the extent of your ability to be attentive to what they have to say.

Naturally humans always run to places they are being understood, so even in terms of a challenge or complications, they would seek your empathic refuge since you tend to understand their interests better. In developing the aura of leadership, this is also very important. Getting a promotion would be easier if you have this effect on your superiors in the workplace.

The Art of Approach

Confidence

Allow your confidence to be visible in all endeavours. Work on getting rid of nervousness and social anxiety by meeting more people and by doing more things involving different groups of people. Social skills are developed through practice. Even the most introverted or timid individual can turn to a pro social influencer when constant practice is involved. The extent of self-belief will be then determined by the amount of confidence being displayed.

Ultimately the value of your opinion is determined by the amount of confidence you have. Make sure you make eye contact when having a conversation.

Make eye contact and maintain it for several minutes. This may not be easy in the beginning but once you put more practice it would become a second nature. Also, your tone is very important in determining the confidence you have in what you are saying.

People don't care much about the confidence you have within yourself, but the confidence you have in what you are saying. Because in the end it determines whether what you are saying is true, false, or exaggerated. You don't need to sound arrogant either. Just be assertive in your opinion and use all the big words necessary to show that you know what you are talking about.

Fraternize Effectively

Friendliness

There is no way you can communicate effectively without showing some extent of friendliness. One way to show people that you are friendly is by asking them personal questions and being interested in their personal stuff. Keeping the smile regular is also very important.

A simple smile can turn strangers into friends and you can usually influence them with your presence. Another way of showcasing friendliness is by encouraging people to be their best even by commending and praising their efforts.

The most important thing in friendliness is to get your target to be honest with you about their feelings. Politeness goes a long way in cultivating better friendship. In a workplace, the more friends you have the easier and faster will you get stuff done. But things get to the best when you cultivate quality friendship.

Talk about their weaknesses, their family and the things they've been complaining about recently. Show that you care about their feelings and that you remember simple details. Everyone wants to feel appreciated in all circumstance, this is where the groundwork of friendship is built.

Clarity and Concision

Communication is not enough, you have to make sure that your communication is precise and concise. You have to balance between talking too little and talking too much. Apparently people may get tired of you easily if you talk too much especially about the same thing.

On the other hand, you have to make sure that you have talked enough to provide clarity on the subject you are trying to discuss. So it is important to ask questions before you convey your opinion or instruction. It is entirely important that you have a definite direction and purpose for initiating a conversation. Few words but concise will always win.

Always go direct to the point after exchanging few pleasantries. In a work setting, it is better to go direct to the point in order to avoid rambling, making your potential allies to get bored and miss the whole point of your message.

People are often distracted, so try as much as possible to make it simple even as you use sensitive words to get their attentions. What you want should be clear. If it involves a proposal in which you are offering a certain benefit, let that also be clear to the receiver. The last you would want is for your receiver to misinterpret your messages. It is always proper to think before uttering the word in order to minimize mistakes and to only communicated the details that needs to be communicated.

Hone Your Nonverbal Communication

Tone, hand gestures, eye contact and body language are a very important part of communication. Your confidence, which is very important, will be determined by how you relax your shoulders, how you use your hands and the way you positon your legs. Simply, you have to be relaxed in order to make the other person feel relaxed and accepted.

Do not fold your arms. Place your hands on your waist in order to showcase concentration in the conversation and the person in question. This way you will become approachable even to strangers.

Also, your tone will determine the kind of response you will get from people. Do not use emotional or silent tones when you are supposed to be excited. Using a different tone to convey a different message will only make the other person uncomfortable about the aim of your conversation. It will either make them feel like they are doing something wrong or that you are not being totally honest.

Keep the eye contact critical and friendly. Look them in the eye to boost their confidence that you are giving them full attention.

Law of attraction: how you look at them will determine how they are going to look at you. People respond to the things you do with your body easily than responding to the things you say. The smoothness, speed and accuracy of the conversation will depend on the little things you do with your eyes, legs, and arms.

Another very important factor of good communication is to be able to read and understand body language. Most of the things we do with our body parts are subconscious but they really define our feelings. Take advantage of that in order to become effective in your communication.

The Better Listener

Listening

The best communicators are actually the best listeners. In fact, the best communication you would ever have is when you talk less, ask the right questions and listen carefully to the details being conveyed. Being selfish in communication is never the best way to get the attention of people towards your interests. You have to show that you are interested in their interests in order to get their attentions on your interests.

People get drawn to people that understand them better. Active listening is an art that you have to learn and practice before you can use effectively in a formal or personal settings. You have to ask open-ended questions so that you would get more details from people. Also, ask more details about the new things they mentioned in their stories.

There are details that only good listeners can get real access to. One way to show that you are listening is to repeat what they just say, even if you have to make some modification. With these you can make friends faster, and even the people that supposed to be your superiors will become your friends.

Be Specific

Always go direct to the point especially when you are requesting something from a very important person. If you are sending an email, make the heading as catchy as the purpose of the email. Shorten the pleasantry and go directly to the specific purpose of the message.

Also, do not circle around details when communicating about something important. Dedicate a particular time for a single discussion and do not drift to other details. If you really want something done, you have to focus on that thing at that time without drifting. This will ensure effectiveness at all levels.

Get Rid of Distractions

Know your distractions and get rid of them. If you want to have a smooth conversation for a longer period of time, make sure you use the right time, where distractions are to the minimum. Shutdown your computer and put your phone on silence. The location for your discussion should also provide for full concentration. Also, make sure that the other person is also less distracted. It is your job to provide all the comfort needed that will put distraction at bay.

Use Script

Always use a script especially for small talk. This is important in order to avoid awkward silences in-between conversations. The script system is very effective among people you don't know well or strangers. Also, when conversing with a superior you have to use the script in order to keep things flowing even as you make them feel important. Talk about recreation, goals, family and the present situation or trends. It is easier to spot the kind of things people are interested in. Put more effort in sharing and obtaining information about things that will benefit you and the other person. Let the entire communication be purposeful, hence the effectiveness.

Other Books by the Same Author

- Persuasion Psychology: How to Influence People (Master the Art of Power and Mind Control Techniques)
- Emotional Intelligence: How to Improve Your IQ, Achieve Self-Awareness and Control Your Emotions
- Happiness Hack: The Beginner's Guide to Happiness
- The Creative Treasures: 100 Creative Ways to Boost Your Creativity, Gain Recognition and Establish Authority
- Memory Improvement Techniques: How to Develop a Brilliant Memory, Recall Things Faster and Achieve a Speedy Learning Ability
- The S.M.A.R.T. Goals: How to Get Rich with No Money or Education
- How to Analyze People: "Reading Body Language Psychology" To Recognize Personality Patterns, Understand People And Gain Influence
- 61 Ways to Attract Women According to 61 Experts: The Ultimate Seduction Guide to

Become the Alpha Male Women Can't Resist, Unlock Her Legs and Make them Fall in Love
- How to Become Successful in Life: Motivational Self Help for Wealth Creation and Life Strategies
- Secrets to a Successful Long-Term Relationship: The Key to a Passionate Marriage and Sex Life
- Self-Discipline Training: Ways to Develop Self-Discipline & Stay Committed to A Routine, No Matter What
- How to Organize Your Life: 10 Habits of Really Organized People
- The Law of Attraction Workbook: How to Attract Abundance of Money, Wealth, Love & Health (Turn Failure into Success)
- Time Management Made Easy: How to Cultivate New Habits, Improve Productivity & Get Things Done

www.ingramcontent.com/pod-product-compliance
Lightning Source LLC
Chambersburg PA
CBHW031515210526
45464CB00007B/2918